SOUTHERN SPACES

FOR BEAUTIFUL LIVING

SOUTHERN SPACES

FOR BEAUTIFUL LIVING

hm | books

hm | books

EDITORIAL

EDITOR Kathleen Johnston Whaley

ART DIRECTOR Tracy Wood-Franklin

CREATIVE DIRECTOR/PHOTOGRAPHY Mac Jamieson

MANAGING EDITOR Lisa Frederick

ASSOCIATE EDITOR Mona Moore

ASSISTANT EDITOR Elizabeth Bonner

EDITORIAL ASSISTANT Grace Haynes

COPY EDITOR Nancy Ogburn

CONTRIBUTING WRITERS Karen Callaway, Lauren Eberle, Andrea Fanning, K. Faith Morgan

CONTRIBUTING STYLISTS Sidney Bragiel, Tracey MacMillan Runnion, Adrienne A. Williams

EDITORIAL CONTRIBUTOR Becky Goff

SENIOR PHOTOGRAPHERS John O'Hagan, Marcy Black Simpson

PHOTOGRAPHERS Jim Bathie, William Dickey, Stephanie Welbourne

CONTRIBUTING PHOTOGRAPHERS Stephen DeVries, George Fiala, Lance Selgo

SENIOR DIGITAL IMAGING SPECIALIST Delisa McDaniel

DIGITAL IMAGING SPECIALIST Clark Densmore

DIGITAL MEDIA

MARKETING DIRECTOR Tricia Wagner Williams

ONLINE EDITOR Courtney McDuff

DIGITAL GRAPHIC DESIGNER Alana Hogg

MARKETING SOLUTIONS Ray Reed

ADMINISTRATIVE

HUMAN RESOURCES DIRECTOR Judy Brown Lazenby

IT DIRECTOR Matthew Scott Holt

DEALER PROGRAM MANAGER Janice Ritter

PRODUCTION ASSISTANT Rachel Collins

Front cover photography by John O'Hagan

hm
hoffmanmedia

CHAIRMAN OF THE BOARD/CEO Phyllis Hoffman DePiano

PRESIDENT/COO Eric W. Hoffman

PRESIDENT/CCO Brian Hart Hoffman

EXECUTIVE VICE PRESIDENT/CFO Mary P. Cummings

EXECUTIVE VICE PRESIDENT/OPERATIONS AND MANUFACTURING Greg Baugh

VICE PRESIDENT/DIGITAL MEDIA Jon Adamson

VICE PRESIDENT/EDITORIAL Cindy Smith Cooper

VICE PRESIDENT/INTEGRATED MARKETING SOLUTIONS Ray Reed

VICE PRESIDENT/ADMINISTRATION Lynn Lee Terry

Hoffman Media
1900 International Park Drive, Suite 50
Birmingham, Alabama 35243
www.hoffmanmedia.com

ISBN # 978-1-940772-33-2
Printed in China

Contents

Introduction

Much like the personalities of homeowners themselves, each room of a Southern house holds its own distinctive identity. There's the welcome that extends from a well-appointed foyer and the invitation that marks a gracious living room, entreating family and visitors to sit and stay awhile. Master suites burst with luxury, guest bedrooms embody hospitality, and children's rooms serve as special places where young imaginations learn to flourish. Kitchens and dining rooms, studies and porches—they all have their own impact on daily life and the overall feel of the dwellings we call home. But the worth of these spaces goes beyond their contrasting roles. Surely, the beauty of design lies in the many unique ways you can color the framework created by a room's central purpose. This book celebrates that notion with room-by-room chapters that offer a rainbow of ideas for interpreting the union between form and function, all with the signature soul of the South. You'll discover a kaleidoscope of preferences and passions that play out to achieve entirely different living, dining, and resting spaces and learn how, together, such thoughtful interiors build a home alive with love and Southern style.

FOYERS

Greetings and salutations! The front door opens wide with welcome, and guests enter with delight and anticipation for what lies ahead. Here in the entryway, hospitality has an opportunity to shine—as does the Southern abode. Whether bedecked in traditional wallpaper or painted with the latest batch of on-trend neutrals, this typically small space can make a big impact and a lasting impression. Hellos and goodbyes linger in the air, remembrances of friends arriving for birthday parties, of generous food-gift deliveries, of sweet embraces under the holiday mistletoe. The foyer is also a prime location for a seasonal showcase. Throughout the year, winter branches frosted in faux snow make way for freshly picked springtime blossoms in a simple vase, and in turn, hunted-and-gathered autumn pinecones are exchanged for the joys of holly and ivy. Ah, what a versatile space and what a lovely place to begin.

Natural light acts as its own design element in this stately entrance, dancing through arched windows and reflecting off limestone floors to bathe its grand staircase. Nestled underneath, a sitting area filled with art and antiques extends the feeling of hospitality.

An intricately carved front door from India sets the tone for a home imbued with Craftsman design and salvage details. Coffered ceilings and gentle archways keep the room airy while softening the expansive interiors. A center table atop a cowhide rug anchors the open-concept space, providing a focal point for the entryway.

Summertime retreats in Nantucket inspired the aesthetic of this Atlanta entry. Light abounds in the understated space, highlighting the barrel ceiling and detailed wainscoting. A lamp fashioned from a colorful Haitian fabric and glass vase brighten the welcoming alcove.

Exposed brick lends texture and architectural interest to a foyer where a pillow-plumped settee invites guests to wait in comfort (left). Just off the entry, a hallway-turned-gallery displays family photographs, with similar mats and frames forming a cohesive grouping. Brightly hued rugs lead to a hall tree holding a collection of walking canes.

Large-paned windows on French-inspired front doors showcase a foyer brimming with special treasures. An abstract painting by Lori Terry complements the collection of blue-and-white pottery and an antique set of pots de crème tucked away on a vintage console. Matching chairs were slipcovered to soften the wooden frames and help draw the eye to herringbone parquet flooring.

This 1934 French home in the heart of Buckhead in Atlanta reflects a contemporary character while staying true to its distinctive architectural identity. Its vivid periwinkle front door, surrounded by espaliered roses and verdant plantings, radiates a warm welcome to all. Inside, a crisp linen-white palette shines beneath an abundance of antique lighting in the entryway and beyond. Plush chairs brightened by coral pillows invite visitors to sit a spell. Floral arrangements and carefully selected artwork add personal touches.

"I love a chest in an entryway. It grounds the space and gives you a place for storage and for displays."

—BETH JORDAN

Homeowner Beth Jordan blended vintage and modern elements in her foyer for a collected sensibility that offsets the polish of new construction. She added moldings around the front door to boost the character of the room and bedecked the recessed niches with weathered statuary. "The statues were actually for a garden, but I liked the look of white on white and how they fit the space," Beth says. A cowhide rug offers an upbeat twist that plays well with the antiques while acting as a bridge between the coffee-colored door and black flooring.

Sunlight floods the foyer through curved doors wrapped in ornamental ironwork, illuminating the interiors of this majestic Bluffton, South Carolina, home. That stunning first impression is underscored throughout the house, which boasts many architectural treasures. The expansive grand gallery (right) spans the river side of the house and features an impressive groin vault ceiling. Standing between the lamps on the hall chest is a large silver epergne, purchased from the estate of explorer Admiral Richard Byrd.

LIVING ROOMS

Author Alexandra Stoddard says, "Make every room a living room." The concept is indeed a precious one. Each day brings with it another opportunity to appreciate blessings and enjoy moments, many of which happen in this aptly named Southern space. The living room is a hub of activity, from bridge club meetings to family movie nights. Here, longtime friends can sit and chat about nothing or everything for hours on end, and little ones can take those first adorable, toddling steps from the sofa to the coffee table. Typically one of the largest spaces in the home, this is where guests can mix and mingle during a fabulous party, and on a Sunday afternoon, it becomes the room where you put your feet up and bask in the simple pleasures of a cozy blanket and a good book. This is living, and it is beautiful.

Bold colors and graphic patterns mix with abstract art and traditional blue-and-white accents to create a timeless space with a contemporary feel. Holding favorite curios, a sleek monogrammed tray on the coffee table increases the Southern appeal.

Patterned textiles, efficient furniture flow, and attention to scale went a long way toward making this room functional—and fun. A palette of blue lays the foundation, but other colors keep the hue from becoming tiring or stale. Heirloom pieces, such as a brilliant antique rug, add history and character to the space. These traditional selections juxtapose with more modern elements, like the Lucite coffee table, for a fresh look.

Traditional elements paired with light-and-fresh accents bring harmony to this living room. With its lovely mix of collected pieces and heirlooms, the space is decidedly elegant, but it keeps an approachable, livable quality for the family. A wash of soft creams and browns helps retain a warm and inviting atmosphere, while patterned upholstery, pillows, and tabletop accessories add subtle personality. "Though I enjoy the opportunity to work in a wide range of aesthetics, my personal style has always been a classic, traditional look," interior designer Sally May says of her approach for this room. "Mixing in a few edgy elements is important to add interest, but I gravitate toward timeless, understated spaces."

On the rear wall, a hand-painted mural on canvas by Mary Ellen Scull creates an intricately detailed focal point for the tailored aesthetic and dignified air that define this living room. Depicting a square in France from a bygone era, the piece inspired the subdued palette carried throughout the room. An asymmetrical seating arrangement—including a pair of unmatched yet harmonious side tables—allows space for a grand piano.

"I love using textural materials for the background of the house and then pops of color and vintage finds for accessories. I'm always mixing old and new pieces together." — LUCY FARMER

With a knack for incorporating storied treasures into each design project, Lucy Farmer filled her own home with an eclectic collection of reclaimed pieces that achieves a comfortably rustic look. This space is composed of an assortment of restored architectural accents— the flooring and the front doors as well as the bricks, corbels, andirons, and beams that make up the mantel and fireplace. From the French glass sculpture atop the console table to the S.A. Maples Studio painting above the mantel, Lucy selected art that provides modern polish.

Designer Kara Cox says styling a bookcase is like completing a puzzle. "You have to keep working until you get the right balance of personal and decorative pieces," she explains. Painted in a soft blue, the back wall of the built-ins warms up this Greensboro, North Carolina, living room and provides a subtle backdrop to the books and family mementos. Roman shades and other accessories in a range of blues and greens carry the coastal theme to shore. Kara made it a point to use fine art, including a fish sculpture and an abstract painting for the mantel (above left), in her design. "The original art we commissioned over the mantel is my favorite part of the room," she says. "I love to expose my clients to original art and help them learn about starting a collection. It is an incredible personal touch to add to a space."

A defining aspect of this inviting urban interior is a powerful wash of gray that reads as clean but not austere. The neutral palette—made rich by ebony-and-espresso-stained beams and floors—suits the unique architecture of the room, as well as the homeowners, who enjoy changing out elements as they find new pieces for their collections. Cool colors presented with rustic panache are balanced by soft furnishings and textiles, like a side table featuring custom details from Pakistan and a pair of ikat-covered chairs. A colorful rug brings vibrant focus to the center of the space.

Relying on soft tones, designer Lisa Gabrielson gracefully blended a range of colors, furthering the light-and-bright feel of this sun-filled space. For a look that balances comfort and sophistication, she brought in seating in assorted styles and hues. Lively patterns and rustic elements lend a note of inviting interest. The layered yellow shades on the walls evoke the storied feel of an Italian villa.

Rather than allow a single theme to drive selections for their home, the owners found a place for the pieces that interested them. Antique frames and art from family travels are displayed on the walls and in tiers above the mantel, resulting in a vignette of favorite historic pieces and mementos. An array of fabrics lend richness to the room, as delicate silks and sateens layer with robust velvet and burlap. Variations of wood and a brick fireplace continue the vivid textural collaboration. Paired with the well-curated collection, the living area feels vibrant and intriguing but not cluttered.

Set against the soothing backdrop of Benjamin Moore's White Dove and Revere Pewter, the hand-hewn ceiling beams are an ideal, organic element in this casual family room. During the day, sunlight flows through the house's tall windows, illuminating the vibrant colors in the cozy rug and fittings. The homeowners selected plush furniture to invite comfort and conversation and added unique accents for personality and polish.

A European influence is evident throughout this dwelling, especially in such architectural features as the arches that define the great room and round windows of filigree ironwork above them. An intricately carved Chinese chair holds court before one of the room's two seating groups, its delicate design matched by an antique rug and a detailed coffee table purchased in south Florida. Limestone surrounds the fireplace and was the material of choice for the flooring in each of the downstairs rooms.

To echo the sunset view seen from the living room of this Alabama lake house, designer Cindy Barganier garnered inspiration from a Mark Dauber photograph that captures the sublime show. The color scheme draws from hues in the display above the fireplace, pulling in the blues and greens of the nearby water and complementing them with hints of orange and yellow. The room achieves a natural aesthetic with pieces ranging from rustic to refined. A cowhide rug layered over sisal adds depth, and flowers from the yard arranged in an oversize clamshell draw attention to the distinctive coffee table made in Peru.

This room was brought to life by the vibrant oil painting—an original by the homeowners—that now sits atop the mantel. The owners brought the piece to their first meeting with Dallas-based designer Elaine Williamson-Romero and told her they wanted the kind of room they imagined would be in the home depicted in the painting. Elaine set to work on a lively space with a widespread palette of colors and patterns, pushing for intriguing contrast without losing continuity. "The bold colors are mixed on a mainly green foundation for optimum support and fluidity," says Elaine. An array of dynamic motifs is balanced by more understated elements, like a subtle zebra print on the draperies.

Rich neutrals in this living area echo the warmth of the wooden millwork and give the space a tenor of calm and contentment. Multiple seating areas boost the room's functionality, from large sofas and a petite armchair to a pair of swivel chairs that face each other across a leather ottoman. Despite the asymmetrical arrangement, the room retains a sense of balance with the sofa centered on the window wall and the twin lamps that flank it.

DINING ROOMS

Raise a glass to this beloved Southern space. For centuries, the act of breaking bread together has been considered both sacred and celebratory, and this is the place where folks gather for precisely that. Oh, how marvelous are the Easter luncheons with honey-glazed ham and deviled eggs, the bridal showers with petits fours and crudité, the Thanksgiving dinner with herb-roasted turkey and all the trimmings—such culinary delights and wonderful memories are enjoyed here. Seated around the table, hand in hand, you offer gratitude for the provision and for those who have gathered. Beneath the sparkling chandelier, a breathtaking centerpiece composed of favorite flowers adorns the table alongside china handed down through generations. History and heritage are a part of the experience in this space, and all who pull up a chair can partake and savor not just the food, but the moment.

Traditional English lines and a light, natural palette give this dining room a classic sensibility. The crystal chandelier evokes a serene airiness in the formal space, while cushions in a cotton-and-linen crewel soften the lines of the cane-back dining chairs.

This dining room showcases elegant examples of the antique light fixtures and fine furnishings incorporated throughout the traditional 1934 home. The combination of old and new pieces supports an aura of timelessness. Flowers from the garden offer a genteel complement to soft blue walls that bring a feeling of serenity.

Interior designer Mandi Smith T of Birmingham used neutral tones and natural finishes to achieve a sense of simplicity and hospitality in this dining room. A well-placed trio of family portraits lends a personal touch to the space, while a grouping of framed nature-themed prints accentuates the chosen color palette. For a hint of panache, the designer layered a complementary pattern along the leading edge of the linen draperies. The slipcovered dining chairs add to the approachable atmosphere, and their easy-to-clean quality makes them a homeowner favorite. Instead of a china cabinet, open industrial shelves hold dishes and serving pieces.

"Since blue almost acts as a neutral, it's a great way to introduce color to clients who aren't used to a lot of it." —EMILY LARKIN

Before Emily Larkin of Dallas-based EJ Interiors got her hands on this dining room, it was covered in nothing but neutrals. "Our main goal was to liven it up with color and create a fresh, modern, and elegant space," she explains. They used the homeowner's antique rug as a starting point for the new color scheme, pulling out its refined navy blue and incorporating it into the chairs. With durability as another goal, they covered the chairs in a sturdy polyester that mimics silk, and this type of practical luxury became the room's mantra.

This room builds on personal collections to create a distinctive space. The design started with a cherished set of 14 antique dining chairs and a collection of Blue Willow porcelain. Both inspired the upholstery of a soft floral fabric on the walls. The print features blue-and-white vases overflowing with flowers. Wrapped in leather with large ornate locks, the buffet resembles a Dutch trunk and underscores the Old-World influence.

A geometric blue-and-green print fabric suggested by designer Alison Smith touched off this room's décor. Subdued celadon walls enhance the pattern and infuse an extra hint of color into the design for an inviting feel. Bought at an architectural antiques shop, the drop-leaf dining table is large in scale, but its compact footprint suits the space.

"The dining room is where 'family' really happens," designer Cindy Barganier says of this Alabama space. She worked with the homeowners to create an elegant yet functional sensibility. A rustic farm table anchors the design, while stately chairs preserve a more formal tone. Artist Marilyn Heard painted the walls in a landscape scene lighthearted enough for the children to imagine woodland animals playing behind the two-dimensional trees. The tailored chair slipcovers feature a fabric called Palette Knife, which Cindy designed.

The artful blend of new and heirloom elements makes this space feel polished and livable. Passed-down antiques like the armoire and buffet continue their journey here, while pieces such as the table were purchased specifically for the house from estate sales. The reproduction chairs are covered in a blue, green, and cream plaid to add a friendly touch to the formal room. The homeowner painted the buffet and then chose a favorite piece of art to hang above it. Mounting the work on a backdrop of wood harvested from the family farm resulted in a more prominent display for the special painting. Place settings featuring Vietri dinnerware further enhance the color scheme and design elements of the space.

This open area has well-defined spaces without
the use of walls. Contrasting yet complementary
area rugs and the use of light fixtures skillfully
delineate the dining room from the hallway.
A mix of furniture pieces gives the impression
of cherished finds collected over time.

Old and new combine beautifully in this dining room, where gilt accents such as the geometric lamps lend sparkle to the carved wooden furnishings and dignified palette. Contrasting fabrics on the shield-back dining chairs, as well as the oriental rug, echo the sapphire-blue walls and balance the hue with notes of rich red. Designers Lathem Gordon and Cate Dunning framed black-and-white photos and family love letters for a personal top note that makes the room an extra-special spot to share meals and stories *en famille*.

"It was important that we allowed the light to flow throughout the spaces. The homeowner is such a happy and gracious lady, and I wanted the home to exemplify her personality." — BEVERLY FARRINGTON

Just off the kitchen, a light-filled breakfast room offers the family a cheerful and informal setting to enjoy meals. Designer Beverly Farrington chose simple cafe curtains in a coral-and-green fabric, paired with wooden blinds, for the expanse of windows offering views of the back garden. She also selected pleated chair skirts in a coordinating material to give weight to the pedestal table.

A few thoughtfully chosen statement pieces can elevate a simple space to be entirely captivating. Such is the case in this understated dining room, where a beaded chandelier—one of the first purchases for the home—appears at once striking and demure. The cream cabinet is also a favorite element because it shows off many of the homeowners' beloved treasures that might otherwise be hidden away. Beneath a gold-flecked Wellon Bridgers painting, a reproduction piece offers another place to display heirlooms, like a tea set passed down from the owner's great-grandparents, while a centerpiece of ornamental oregano in an antique jardinière presents one more example of the outstanding result that comes from marrying ease and elegance.

Dallas-based interior designer Amy Gibbs paired traditional furnishings with spectacular accent pieces to create a bright, updated French-country design. The homeowner fell in love with a raw amethyst bowl that weighs nearly 50 pounds and found a place for it as a centerpiece on the dining room table. A gilded mirror spotted on an antiquing trip to Pennsylvania reflects a peacock painting by C. Hagop-Ian that hangs on the opposite wall. These treasures all shine beneath a reproduction chandelier.

KITCHENS

The kitchen is the heart of the Southern home. This room, which underscores the need for form as well as function, is both a literal and figurative hot spot—no matter the size, it's where guests and loved ones tend to flock. Conversations flow easily in this special space, perhaps because of the engaging combination of artistry and labor involved in cooking a meal. On leisurely mornings, family and overnight guests alike climb out of bed and follow their noses to the sizzling bacon and rising cinnamon rolls that await. On any given day, fresh vegetables from the farmers' market may fill a bowl on a marble-top island, as bar stools provide the perfect perch for curious onlookers who will inevitably want to help stir the cake batter—and lick the spoon. Modern conveniences reveal signs of the times, but the secret ingredient for a remarkable kitchen has been and always will be warmth and love.

Dramatic double-box pendants and white-leather bar stools present a dash of glamour in this bright and cheery Birmingham kitchen. Reclaimed wood paneling on the range hood tones down the formality and adds a textural top note.

This Dallas kitchen features a herringbone-pattern backsplash formed from pieces of antique Chicago bricks chosen by the home's original designer, Linda Lehman. Designer Amy Gibbs freshened up the space with local touches like the wrought-iron light fixture, which she found at Crow Chandeliers in the Dallas Design District. The hand-scraped oak floors throughout the home are low maintenance—perfect for the active lifestyle of the homeowners and their three children. Built-in refrigerator drawers in the island offer the little ones easy access to snacks and beverages.

When Kelley Norwood and her family of five began a full renovation nearly two years ago, their 1990s home had some telltale signs of age. Now that they've replaced wallpaper, a mirrored backsplash, and painted flooring with an updated design, the Norwoods' sun-splashed kitchen is both functional and stylish. The island area underwent a full overhaul, from the selection of statement pendant lighting to the extended surface top with magnificent marble that appears in motion. Kelley also supplanted an awkward desk with a homey hutch that includes rows of accessible storage. In the breakfast nook, a custom banquette adds extra-soft and sophisticated seating.

As art aficionados, the homeowners found ways to display favorite pieces throughout the home, and the kitchen is no exception. The moss-green glaze of the cabinetry brings restrained color to the space, where tole trays and majolica plates sit atop counters. A bow-front sink is set into a soapstone-topped island, and marble tile is laid in an eye-catching harlequin pattern to form the backsplash.

In this galley-style layout, the key ingredient is natural light. Tall windows let the sunshine in, and white cabinetry helps reflect the rays. Together they give the not-so-large room a spacious, airy feel. Open shelving made from reclaimed wood lends a rustic vibe; sleek hardware adds a modern tone; and an undermount farmhouse sink borrows from both styles, unifying the look.

"Modern Farmhouse" was the aesthetic Darren Hearsch and his family embraced when they built their home. "We wanted a large, functional kitchen with both modern lines and a rustic feel," the Decatur, Georgia, resident recalls. An antique white-oak island—fashioned from a support beam from a 1900s barn—is the centerpiece of the space, as well as a grand gathering place for family and guests. Reclaimed open shelving adds visual appeal and, as a bonus, Darren adds, costs less than cabinets. Meanwhile large statement art and colorful kitchen accessories add liveliness to this heart of the home.

"This kitchen was always very pretty. I tried to keep the 'pretty' but bring it to life. I replaced the lights, repainted some areas, and turned the attached breakfast room into a fabulous family gathering area." —MERIDY KING

Knowing the family would enjoy most breakfasts seated at the island, designer Meridy King repurposed the adjacent breakfast nook as a sunroom where the family could entertain and enjoy company. She then tied the spaces together with versatile outdoor fabrics in modern prints. The hard, utilitarian lines of glass-and-metal kitchen lights add an engaging contrast with the soft, beaded fabric of the sunroom's fixture.

This bucolic kitchen comes together with an assemblage of restored resources. Reclaimed flooring flows throughout the space with boards that hold an interesting Southern heritage—originally from a mid-1800s general store in Tennessee. The island, its corbels, and the pendants hanging above all boast salvaged materials as well. Handmade terra-cotta tiles create a honeycomb effect on the accent wall behind the range. Colorful dishes on display, as well as fresh fruit and flowers, bring warmth to the rustic setup, brightening the scene.

The geometric tile backsplash, which balances the large wooden range hood, inspired the design of this elegant kitchen. Its spacious floor plan allows ample seating, both at the oversize island and at the custom banquette that curves to clear a walkway. Generous, layered lighting and banks of pale cabinetry help prevent the dark woods from feeling too heavy.

A crisp White Dove paint coats every inch of this coastal cottage, creating the perfect backdrop for art and accessories that can easily be swapped throughout the year. Hues of blue—navy, royal, sky, and more—offer a cheerful nod to homeowner Lauren Welden's childhood abode, where every room contained a tinge of blue, in either a lamp, pillow, wallpaper, or frame. In the modest kitchen, collectibles ranging from pretty plates to practical glassware are tucked away but on display in a smart storage nook that sports the favored hue. At once kitschy and sweetly nostalgic, the folk art–styled "kitchen lady" from Lauren's sister is a creative assemblage of their mother's beloved cooking utensils.

This kitchen balances the New Orleans–style family room just beyond. Its more subdued color scheme provides a relaxed dining experience while still pulling in the palette of its vibrant counterpart in a few key places. The custom-designed table and banquette, as well as the cabinets that flank them, were planned with optimum seating in mind. Unexpected details, such as purple pendant lights and barstools with unique glass insets, bring interest to the crisp white kitchen.

In a modest bungalow kitchen anchored by dark cabinetry, framed artwork adds splashes of color, while a transom, needlework chair cushions, and bud vases along the windows highlight its cottage charm. A well-worn butler's pantry holds the family's heirloom china collection, protecting the kinds of historical pieces that are among the owner's favorites.

The vision for this design started with one statement piece: a grand gray cabinet, which the homeowner saw in a magazine and loved. Also high on her wish list were a wood-top island, lots of seating for the family's four children, and the biggest farm sink possible.

MASTER BEDROOMS

The hours between sunrise and sunset often consist of the daily grind, and come nightfall, the need for retreat is real. Enter the master bedroom, a place of relaxation, refuge, and rest—a place of your very own. Sumptuous bedding and wall colors in calming palettes invite you to escape from the busyness and exhale. Personal preferences reign supreme in this realm, perhaps more so than in any other room in the house, and as monarch, your design decrees are the only ones that matter. Here, a complete collection of Jane Austen books can be considered as much a necessity as a bedside table—the beauty of the decision is that it is entirely up to you. All around are favorite things: family pictures, framed artwork, flea-market finds. Whether soft and romantic or chic and sophisticated, this Southern space is all about solace.

For this room, designer Cindy Barganier envisioned an upscale getaway for the busy mom and dad. With a custom iron canopy bed and an elegant chandelier, the couple acquired a private space that feels worlds apart from the demands of everyday life.

An intricate botanical fabric sets the framework for this Tennessee master bedroom, which features an assemblage of accents and details that underline a Southern pedigree. The Axminster rug, loomed in England, was a splurge. Its blue-and-winter-white wool provides softness and warmth on a cold morning. Resting atop a painted dresser, a dreamy landscape complements the room's mix of earth tones and floral motifs.

The homeowner achieved an approachable look by choosing pieces with a sense of history—most notably a pair of antique lamps inherited from her great-aunt and updated with black shades. She integrated classic pieces like a sleigh bed and a set of antique nesting tables with a modern shag rug. A brown-and-gold crushed-velvet sofa has become a favorite place to relax and soak in the sun.

"This room was Paris inspired and, with the textile treatments, just speaks Paris to me. I like to be soothed by fabric. This is my little haven." —CATERINA MEADOWS

From the cream diamante matelassé bedding to the brown-and-moss harlequin headboard and bedskirt, designer Caterina Meadows took her inspiration from the City of Light. A bed crown draped in complementing tones completes the romantic scheme, and custom-framed silhouettes and an antique bedside table contribute to the design.

In this master suite, an artful mix of pieces from around the world work together to create a distinctive salvage style. The rustic warmth of an A-frame ceiling covered in pecky cypress brings out the resplendent artistry of the headboard, fashioned out of stained glass recovered from an 1890 chapel in Florida. A blending of patterns and textures helps the mostly neutral palette appear more dynamic. A few personal knickknacks, like a stack of relaxing reads topped with antlers and custom-made jewelry, provide decorative accents with a lived-in feel that suits this cozy space.

The inspiration for this enchanting bedroom came in the form of a quaint French floral print. "It was all about the fabric," says designer Patricia McLean. Lending its delightfully feminine pattern to draperies, bedding, and upholstery, the colorful fabric offers a palette of blues, greens, and yellows that feels at once timeless and fresh.

This room's décor centers on a love of family—
from sentimental photos lining the nightstand
to a watercolor above the bed to a collection of
plates bearing mother-and-child motifs. A desk
overlooking the garden serves as a peaceful place
to keep up with correspondence, and an antique
rug ties together the delicate color palette.

This bedroom is a lesson in detailing. Designers Annie Goldberg and Ginny Maguire trimmed charcoal curtain panels with square platinum studs, corded a bench with emerald-green velvet, and wrapped door handles in matching green leather. With the removal of a hall door, the adjoining study became a private hideaway— the perfect place for unwinding after a long day.

Georgia-based designer Lisa Gabrielson made this master suite into the epitome of a rustic retreat. Inspired by mountain cabins, she used calming creams paired with punchy shades of red in the bed linens, fabrics, and sizable flat-weave rug. Shiplap-style walls provided the ideal backdrop for this inviting space, which features a king-size antique poster bed and a gallery-style display made up of flea-market and antique finds. To help keep the look casual, Lisa used playful stripes and preppy paisleys throughout the room. She finished the "collected-over-time vibe" by including mismatched tables, repurposed chairs, and a few houseplants.

An intricately designed bed made in Portugal became the starting point in creating a carefully crafted aesthetic of luxury in this master suite. Pale blue walls set a soothing tone, which is complemented by blue-and-aqua linens and upholstery. Throughout the space, a sense of grandeur comes across in the antique furniture, well-appointed vanity, and artistic decorations. The chair, ottoman, accent table, and lamp were all family heirlooms, updated with the addition of Annie Sloan paint to bring a modern touch and continue the color scheme. Other pieces were incorporated with both style and utility in mind. The marble bust of a young girl displays favorite necklaces in an artful way that also enables convenient accessorizing. The skirted bedside tables were custom made to hide storage for spare blankets and quilts.

A hint of Hollywood Regency glamour boosts this bedroom's panache, creating a look that is simultaneously spunky and serene. Despite the opulent gleam of the headboard, picture framing, and wall mirrors, the medley of luxe materials and the restrained palette create a sense of sink-right-in softness. A set of pearlized oval nightstands adds a bit of polish and serves as the perfect stage for custom lamps made with natural rose quartz. At the foot of the bed, an acrylic bench covered in Mongolian lamb fur brings a final whimsical note. The elegance extends to a dreamy closet that includes ample custom cabinetry faced with antique mirror. The chandelier tops off the space with its square-cut crystal arms and vintage brass elements.

GUEST BEDROOMS

The art of hospitality has long been a Southern specialty. Treating visitors as guests of honor is a practice that easily translates to the design of a guest room, and with a bit of time and intentionality, this space can become one of the most beautiful rooms in the house. Writer Henri Nouwen said, "Hospitality is not to change people, but to offer them space where change can take place." With that in mind, you can make the guest quarters a getaway filled with thoughtful touches and creative ideas to foster relaxation. The overarching goal is to make the space as inviting and as comfortable as possible. When in-laws or former college roommates come to visit, this is their home within your home, which gives you all the more reason to craft the room into the kind of space that extends welcome and exudes joy.

Custom built-ins provide plenty of storage and also form a shallow alcove, perfect for positioning the bed. With space at a premium, wall sconces replace tables and lamps, while pillows offer personality in the otherwise neutral interior.

A bed re-covered with embroidered crewel linen creates a focal point in the room and extends a welcoming, homespun feel. The vintage pine nightstand is painted a warm coral to tie together complementary floral curtains and feminine plaid bedding.

Designer Eric Ross decided to make a bold statement in a guest room the homeowners' grandchildren often use. "I picked a theme of linking geometrics that gave the room a younger feel and made it a little fresher," he says. The geometrics are repeated on the linens, draperies, and carpeting. Pieces from the homeowners' existing blue-and-white collection complete the look.

A trio of vintage terrier prints inspired Fido-friendly décor in this cheerful bedroom. The cherry-red color scheme is carried out from ceiling to floor, with French-inspired fabric used for curtains and bedding. The canine theme continues with a toile Scottie pillow and a pair of needlepoint pups.

The crisp lines of twin campaign beds in
this guest room offset the ornate mirror.
"Antiques and today's furniture bring out
the best in each other," says designer
Carter Kay. The needlepoint chair and
the scalloped dressing table, which
substitute for conventional nightstands,
belonged to the homeowner's mother.

Part Asian, part modern, and one hundred percent fun, this colorful room channels a classic black-and-white color combination, splashed with liberal doses of salmon. A faux-zebra rug placed at an angle beneath the bed is echoed in the contemporary art on the wall. In contrast to the crisp white duvet, a black tassel-trimmed throw drapes across the bed, while a grouping of pillows, in both solids and prints, brightens up the wooden headboard. At the foot of the bed, a pair of leather stools with hobnail detail are both chic and useful—the perfect perches for tying shoes or placing small pieces of travel gear.

"This space is definitely one of my most favorite in the house—it's happy and fun." —HEATHER WILLIAMS

Homeowner Heather Williams's sister, who lives in Mexico, commissioned a local artisan to hand-draw and stitch the animal-themed tapestry fabric for this bedroom. Fashioned into headboards, the fabric lends just enough punch without overwhelming the space. Brilliant orange and emerald green bring a sense of energy that's tempered by the cream-and-beige backdrop.

Staying true to the architectural style of this home, a guest room bears the elegant characteristics of Victorian design. Trellis-patterned wallpaper in a pretty powder-blue shade forms the backdrop for a headboard covered in bright floral fabric. Window treatments pull the peach hues from the pillows, and box-pleat valances give the draperies a formal, finished look. Artwork evokes Victorian-era scenes, and a favorite chair, reupholstered in ecru linen and adorned with gold fabric trim, makes a cozy spot for reading or enjoying a cup of tea.

CHILDREN'S BEDROOMS

Baby beds. Rocking chairs. *Goodnight Moon*. Winnie the Pooh. Fairytales and lullabies. Growth charts. Race cars. Trains and planes. Pink ponies. Princess dresses. Doodles and dollhouses. The wonders of childhood are many, and the season is priceless. A child's bedroom is his or her fortress, clubhouse, and secret hideout. Full of whimsy, the walls play along and help lend an air of hope and vibrancy to the space. Themes are popular picks for these rooms, and the options are limitless. What fun! Red, blue, white. Yellow and green. Color can do so much to help make the area feel fresh and youthful. Artwork, toys, and shelves laden with trophies and medals. This space is both an archive and a classroom. Tucked into their beds all snug as a bug in a rug, little ones need only look around their room to find great inspiration.

Bedecked in ribbons and ruffles, this lovely-in-lavender nursery offers tranquil surroundings for sweet slumber. A quilted monogram hanging and custom bedding and window treatments are at the center of the space's precious details.

A playful fox-themed fabric highlights this nursery, which works for either a bouncing boy or girl and can transition easily beyond the infant years. Holli Zollinger of Spoonflower, where the fabric was sourced, worked with designers Leigh Pate and Caterina Meadows to create a complementary print for the Roman shade and other details. Sliding barn doors need only a small footprint to conceal storage space. Ruffled detailing softens the burlap curtains, while whimsical animal-themed artwork carries through the fabric motif.

An heirloom white iron bed was the starting point for a dreamy room fit for a princess. Custom-made shams and a button-trimmed, monogrammed pillow offer frilly accents to a pink skirt and white quilted coverlet. On the window, floral draperies are topped with a lace valance made from antique tablecloths, further balancing the playful space with vintage details.

This charming little girl's room exudes whimsy with a motif rooted in both magical and natural splendor—from the fairytale-themed artwork by Liesl Long to the dragonfly figurines made by a Florida artisan out of old porch rails, ceiling-fan blades, and plumbing parts. The color scheme incorporating blue, pink, and dashes of yellow creates a happy space for a growing girl to call her own. The room also lends itself to uncomplicated transition, allowing for simple accent changes as the child and her tastes mature. Timeless fixtures—like the passed-down beds and nightside table—offer flexibility through the years.

Fostering daughter Annie's lifelong passion for art has always been both a priority and a pleasure for homeowner Jeramy Neill. For Annie's bedroom, the family chose a white built-in art desk and stately antique easel. Encouraging hours of creative endeavors leads to many masterpieces and walls filled with colorful collages. When dreamtime comes, the young artist rests on a bed piled with pillows, which she helped select, under a neutral headboard covered with durable ostrich vinyl. Against the wall, a sweet love seat is a nostalgic piece from Jeramy's own childhood bedroom—the perfect place to sit and doodle with a sketch pad and pencils.

"I wanted to create a beautiful oasis for our family to come home to on a daily basis—one that is filled with both old family memories and new ones we're making now." —JERAMY NEILL

This four-poster bed, passed down from homeowner Jeramy Neill's grandmother, serves as an anchor for a room that exemplifies a layered look. Accessories like antlers and a driftwood mirror are nods to nature that also lend a more masculine mood. Vintage suitcases are a clever solution for stashing toys, beloved books, or other mementos while keeping them in easy reach.

Sturdy wood furnishings lend visual weight to this otherwise airy space and stand up to wear and tear. A striped coverlet and a diamond-motif shag rug introduce pattern yet preserve the room's boyish feel, and a slender chaise makes an ideal spot for downtime with a book. Throw pillows bearing dog silhouettes are a sweet tribute to loyal childhood companions.

BATHROOMS

When measured in square feet, the bathroom is often a tiny fraction of the overall house plan. However, with a good design plan, it can add exponential value to the appeal of your abode. Thoughtfully appointed powder rooms can extend the feeling of hospitality for your guests, but they also give you an opportunity to experiment with style. Because the space is small, you can splurge on the flocked wallpaper you've admired for years or try out that vibrant paint color that keeps catching your eye. Faucets, fixtures, and hardware are fairly minimal updates that yield maximum impact. In the master suite, the bathroom can go beyond functionality and act as a private spa. Color palette options are plentiful, so you can keep things calm or go bold. From clean and modern to traditional and stately, the spectrum of ways to decorate is broad—and so is the array of possibilities to unwind.

Wall coverings lend a luminous quality to this master bath. Its subtle chinoiserie toile shimmers from the room's natural light and polished-nickel sconces. Carrara marble floors echo matching countertops and exude a sense of luxury. A floor bench finished in silver leaf and a gold glaze completes the soothing space.

In this master bath, artisanal accents elevate a traditional design. Owners of Roman Brantley Art & Antiques in Birmingham, the homeowners had ideas for this room long before they renovated it. "We are avid collectors," says Linda Brantley, "and we built the space around some of our favorite pieces." Linda came across an artist in Louisiana who made reproduction stained glass in the classic Tiffany style. "His work was so beautiful, and he even signed it for us," she says. The stunning stained-glass window depicting a majestic mountain vista became a showpiece in the room. The couple searched for a contemporary bathtub that suited the scale, and in lieu of using expensive stone as the base for it, Linda called upon a local craftsman to cast a concrete base that would resemble stone—a budget-friendly solution. Wood cabinetry, crown molding, and a two-way mirror-television to which she added antique framework helped unify the look. The Brantleys also brought in a beloved 10-foot French cabinet to anchor the wall opposite the vanity, and then came the *pièce de résistance*: a handcrafted, primarily pink chandelier found at an estate sale decades before.

Soaring arched windows and antique candelabras create a personal sanctuary full of serenity and grandeur. Aged doors, custom cabinetry, and carved mirror frames combine for a rustic European look filled with Old-World charm and modern-day appeal.

A duo of delicately scalloped his-and-hers mirrors steals the show in this coastal master bathroom, adding superb style and an interesting twist to an otherwise casual space. The hand-painted, avian-themed mirrors came with the house and tie in nicely with icy-blue accents. Richly honed brown marble countertops complement the trio of baskets below, which brim with plush white bath towels. These textured storage solutions hide a pretty yet functional secret: The homeowners trimmed the backs of the baskets to slide around and disguise unsightly sink pipes and a wooden support. The result is a room full of mixed metals and tons of textures, an idyllic retreat within the owners' suite.

*"We wanted the master bath to be really special,
so we mixed a little French style with classic
Victorian. The result is truly elegant in every way."*

—BEVERLY FARRINGTON

Rather than install standard built-in cabinetry,
designer Beverly Farrington opted for a custom-
made armoire with mirrored-glass inserts and
his-and-hers marble-topped vanities. The
armoire and antique trumeau mirrors, placed
over the vanities, reflect incoming sunlight to
keep the room bright and airy. Black and white
floor tiles offer a clean vintage look, while floral
wallpaper adds a formal and feminine touch.

Because this guest bathroom is small in scale, the homeowner wanted to create the illusion of greater space. She chose a tree-patterned wallpaper with strong vertical lines that help draw the eye upward and added a red chinoiserie mirror for a bit of color and pizzazz. Brass fixtures pick up the gold hue of the pears on the wallpaper. Monogrammed towels and a handful of vibrant fresh flowers signal a warm welcome to visitors.

To anchor this powder room, designer Libby Greene felt that more than a pedestal sink was needed, so she found an old French piece and traded its original top for classic travertine. To complement the refinement of the fixture, she selected a painted antique trumeau mirror to hang above it and flanked the mirror with a pair of petite sconces.

With their diminutive jewel-box feel, powder baths can be ideal places to introduce bold or unusual materials. Deep marine-blue walls and a colorful pendant (left) infuse this bath with drama, while a roughly hewn sink (right) acts as the focal point in an otherwise simple space.

STUDIES & LIBRARIES

There is something poetic and full of promise about a room set aside for learning. Writer Jorge Luis Borges said, "I have always imagined that Paradise will be a kind of library." And famed poet and playwright T. S. Eliot said, "The very existence of libraries affords the best evidence that we may yet have hope for the future of man." Indeed, a study or a library can provide the most incredible opportunities to discover, converse, and create. From rugged and rustic to polished and posh, style in this type of room tends to run the gamut and often carries a hint of global influence—rightfully so, since the novels contained here often include daring adventures in interesting places. Even working amid this kind of atmosphere produces a sort of nostalgic excitement, and it doesn't take long to adopt the same opinions about these spaces as did the greats who have gone before.

Sometimes the best unifying factor in a collection is simply the fact that the owner loves every piece and is drawn to it. There is little commonality in this gallery-style grouping, but together they relate the travels, adventures, and life of their owner.

Inspiration abounds in the form of lively patterns, shimmering metallics, and vibrant colors in the North Carolina home office of Cheryl Luckett. A boldly striped black-and-white rug anchors the room, and as this rainbow-festooned space demonstrates, white walls needn't indicate a monochromatic or subdued result. This clean background acts as a canvas for an artistic compilation of the many trinkets and treasures the homeowner has collected over years of decorating work. Even the signs of her trade—a bouquetlike assembly of fabric bolts in the corner and design books on the shelves—add to the stylish ambiance of the space. Hints of classic and traditional touches with tongue-in-cheek flair ground the contemporary room, and the abundant window light makes this the perfect workroom for the color and materials selections necessary in her design role.

From personal correspondence to keeping track of the family's busy schedule, this home office acts as the hub of the household. But style is not sacrificed for function. Artistic accents, such as original paintings and a collection of white vases, highlight the seamless polish of a custom wall unit.

A mother of four with a full house and a full life, Jan Ware knew she needed an office that would make coming to work a pleasure. Detached from her house, this sun-splashed space with a small kitchen niche is just the ticket for the owner of Jan Ware Designs. A clean, contemporary palette of white shiplap and neutral furnishings is a soothing start for a day filled with fabric samples and paint swatches. Statement pieces like an antique iron fixture and a striking desk showcase Jan's skill at mixing and matching eras and styles. "The natural light and soothing setting make it easier to focus on client designs from what feels like my own little hideaway," she reveals.

A palette anchored by mocha walls and matching draperies lends a rich, traditional feel to this library—the ideal spot to curl up with a cup of tea. Family portraits and collectibles personalize the room, while accents of red and blue provide depth and texture. A small tapestry, originally bought as a Christmas display, has become a year-round backdrop against an ornate fireplace screen.

"The room is rich and comfortable and inviting, and it's kind of a night room—you want to sit in there and talk about your day. It's just very cozy and warm." —CARTER KAY

Designer Carter Kay drew upon the homeowners' extensive array of family heirlooms and personal treasures—from porcelain and pottery to antiques and fine art—to give this library a mix of seasoned comfort and contemporary flair. A tapestry chair, an equine sculpture, and a lamp mounted on an acrylic base combine to layer interesting artistry into the space.

Growing up in Nashville, this homeowner cherished her parents' soaring library, filled with dark paneling and fine furnishings. When the time came to design her own home, she wanted to incorporate those nostalgic notes into a study that would encourage a lifelong love of learning. Shelves showcase a curated balance of belongings, from framed keepsakes to rare volumes. A Hickory Chair sofa, an antique marble cocktail table, and a pair of leather chairs create a welcoming grouping for conversation, while a high-back club chair takes a sunny spot in the corner, perfect for solo sojourns into a good book.

PORCHES

There's no better view than the one from your own front porch. Oh, to sit in the swing as the rhythmic creak of rocking back and forth becomes a part of the summertime symphony of crickets and cicadas. The sunlight fades to evening, and fireflies dance across the yard. Neighbors drop by for a visit, finding plenty of seating options and a few plump pillows, and they stay for a while and rest a spell. Life is simple here. Seasons change, and you bring out the blankets. Mugs of apple cider are now part of the picture, as are harvest decorations and autumn blooms. The holidays bring good cheer in the form of evergreen and twinkle lights, and wintertime declares less is more by way of décor. But throughout the year, one thing never changes: The Southern porch is a cherished haven.

While still open to the breeze and sunshine, this porch achieves roomlike intimacy through the gingerbread accents and rose-covered trellises. Instead of a traditional fern, a hanging basket of Wandering Jew mirrors the vibrant purple, green, and gray paint colors used on the exterior of this folk Victorian home.

Reclaimed wood gives this newly constructed screened porch a feeling of history and heritage. Embracing the idea of outdoor living, the homeowners considered comfort and durability in their picks for furnishings and accents. In lieu of a traditional porch swing, they opted for a handmade swing bed painted in a robust shade of red, and it has quickly become one of the family's favorite places to perch. A pleasing combo of rattan and rust appears in the selection of side chairs, and the addition of pillows, trays, and a rustic wall clock gives the space a most inviting air that beckons folks to linger longer.

This open pavilion with a coffered ceiling and stone-tiled floors connects the main house to a carriage house and offers views of an exquisite rose garden. The pink fabric of the cushions was chosen to mimic the hues of the roses in bloom. Multiple seating groups divide the expansive space into intimate areas and accommodate a variety of uses.

"Comfort should be at the forefront of Southern design. It's all about relaxing and enjoying the company of others." —TROY RHONE

Leading out from the kitchen, this spot is the first invitation to a backyard oasis sheltered by trees and defined by a series of parterres and patios. Garden designer Troy Rhone worked with the team at Terrebonne Landscape Architectural Design to craft a hand-carved limestone focal point that would break up the expansive red brick wall. The homeowners use the complementary built-in limestone buffet for easy service of cocktails and hors d'oeuvres.

This screened-in porch is original to its 1930s Atlanta home and even includes its fan from that era. The homeowner's love of color—especially blue—influenced the space. A white palette supports a broad spectrum of blues and greens, and a mix of patterns enhances the vibrancy of the scheme. Unique glass accents interspersed with a variety of fresh flowers add textural interest to the room. Highlighting a distinctive wall niche, also original to the porch, is Benjamin Moore's Surf City accentuated by 'Weigela' blooms from the homeowner's garden. Each element works together to create an aesthetic of chic comfort with pieces that exude high-style yet encourage laidback living.

Nestled into the home's rear brick exterior, a cozy patio creates a natural flow from the kitchen to a manicured garden of boxwoods and native Italian plants. The blue painted ceiling brings an old Deep-South tradition into the present and, positioned atop stately white columns, enlarges the feel of the small footprint.

On this poolside patio, impressive stonework forms a grand alfresco setting. Natural elements seen in fixtures and accessories complement the stone walls. Mostly neutral furnishings are enlivened with pieces like grass-green chairs that echo the lush outdoors, as well as classic blue accents that reflect the waterfront vibe the expansive pool creates.

Soaring windows and French doors lead to the terrace of this Charleston condo, which overlooks a central courtyard and offers lovely views of the Ashley River. Lavish potted plants help create the impression of a garden and tie in the greenery that grows outside the building.

Well-planned porches become four-season havens for outdoor living. Take this space, for instance, where a weathered table and chairs create a welcoming gathering place for alfresco meals. Conversation is fostered by the fireplace, where a grouping of casual seating and plush pillows can lead to sipping and story-swapping well into the night. Here, recessed nooks display firewood in a fashionable manner.

A thoughtful design that marries the outdoors to this Dallas home's most commonly used spaces provides its owners year-round enjoyment. At the entrance, a stone pathway links the front door to an adjacent porch that creates a greater sense of privacy than does a traditional layout. Paved with irregular pieces of Pennsylvania flagstone, lined with French doors, and framed with wood posts, the front-porch space evokes the comfortable, welcoming feel of a Texas ranch. The back patio echoes these same elements, adding an outdoor cooking space alongside the swimming area. On cool evenings, the family opens all four sets of back-porch doors and listens to the soothing sounds of the waterfalls around the pool.

Acknowledgments

FOYERS
Cindy Barganier of Cindy E. Barganier Interiors, LLC., 12-13
Meridy King of Meridy King Interiors, 14-15 and 20-21
Jean Anderson and Judy Kyser of Designers Two, 16-17

LIVING ROOMS
GordonDunning, 26
Emily Johnston Larkin of EJ Interiors; Lance Selgo (photographer), 28-29
Sally May of Sally May Interiors, 30-31
Mary Mac & Company, 32-33
Lucy Farmer of Lucy's Inspired, 35
Kara Cox of Kara Cox Interiors, 36-37
Jackie Gooding of Good House Accents, 38-39
Lisa Gabrielson of Lisa Gabrielson Interior Design, 40-41
Michael Eric Dale (designer); Pankey Building Company, 44-45
Cindy Barganier of Cindy E. Barganier Interiors, LLC., 48-49
Elaine Williamson-Romero of Elaine Romero Designs, 50-51
Carter Kay Interiors, 52-53

DINING ROOMS
Meridy King of Meridy King Interiors, 54 and 56-57
Mandi Smith T of Mandi Smith T Interiors, 58-59
Emily Johnston Larkin of EJ Interiors; Lance Selgo (photographer), 60
Eric Ross of Eric Ross Interiors, 62-63
Alison Smith Interiors; Byrom Building Corp., 64-65
Cindy Barganier of Cindy E. Barganier Interiors, LLC, 66-67 and 68-69
Melissa Salem (designer); Kevin Kennemur Construction, 70-71
GordonDunning, 72-73
Beverly Farrington of Accents of the South, 75
Amy Gibbs of Amy Gibbs Interiors, 78-79

KITCHENS
Alison Smith Interiors; Byrom Building Corp., 80
Amy Gibbs of Amy Gibbs Interiors, 82-83
Melanie Pounds Interior Designs, 84-85
Beverly Farrington of Accents of the South, 86-87
Blue Door Design Studio, 88-89
Fletcher Horn of Antique Building Materials, Inc. (woodworker: island, shelves), 90-91
Meridy King of Meridy King Interiors, 92
Lucy Farmer of Lucy's Inspired, 94-95
Meagan Murphree of L&M Interior Design; Korey Webb Construction, 96-97
Virginia Volman Designs, 98-99
Elaine Williamson-Romero of Elaine Romero Designs, 100-101

MASTER BEDROOMS
Cindy Barganier of Cindy E. Barganier Interiors, LLC, 106 and 114-115
Eric Ross of Eric Ross Interiors, 108-109
Caterina Meadows of Pate-Meadows Designs, 113
Lucy Farmer of Lucy's Inspired, 116-117
Patricia McLean of Patricia McLean Interiors, Inc., 118-119
Annie Bayer Goldberg and Ginny Monheit Maquire of AG Interior Designs, 122-123

Lisa Gabrielson of Lisa Gabrielson Interior Design, 124-125
Elaine Williamson-Romero of Elaine Romero Designs, 126-127

GUEST BEDROOMS
Beverly Farrington of Accents of the South, 128
Eric Ross of Eric Ross Interiors, 130-131 and 132-133
Jean Anderson and Judy Kyser of Designers Two, 134-135
Carter Kay Interiors, 136-137
Caterina Meadows of Pate-Meadows Designs, 138-139
Beverly Farrington of Accents of the South, 142-143

CHILDREN'S BEDROOMS
Camren Parrish Interiors, 144
Pate-Meadows Designs, 146-147
Cindy Barganier of Cindy E. Barganier Interiors, LLC, 150-151
Virginia Volman Designs, 152-153 and 155
Alison Smith Interiors; Byrom Building Corp., 156-157

BATHROOMS
Patricia McLean of Patricia McLean Interiors, Inc., 158
Virginia Volman Designs, 164-165
Beverly Farrington of Accents of the South, 166
Libby Greene of Libby Greene Interiors, 169
Melissa Salem (designer), 171

STUDIES & LIBRARIES
Lisa Gabrielson of Lisa Gabrielson Interior Design, 172
Cheryl Luckett of Dwell by Cheryl Interiors, 174-175
Michael Eric Dale (designer); Pankey Building Company, 176-177
Jan Ware of Jan Ware Designs, LLC., 178-179 and 184-185
Carter Kay Interiors, 182

PORCHES
Fletcher Horn of Antique Building Materials, Inc. (woodworker: swing bed), 188-189
Beverly Farrington of Accents of the South, 190-191
Troy Rhone (garden designer); Terrebonne Landscape Architectural Design, 193
Meridy King of Meridy King Interiors, 194-195
Lisa Gabrielson of Lisa Gabrielson Interior Design, 196-197
Emily Johnston Larkin of EJ Interiors; Lance Selgo (photographer), 198-199
Byrom Building Corp., 202-203
Amy Gibbs of Amy Gibbs Interiors, 204-205

TITLE & END PAGES
Meridy King of Meridy King Interiors, 1
Alison Smith Interiors; Byrom Building Corp., 1
Eric Ross of Eric Ross Interiors, 1
Melanie Pounds Interior Design, 2
Carter Kay Interiors, 4-5
Emily Johnston Larkin of EJ Interiors; Lance Selgo (photographer), 6-7
Michael Eric Dale (designer); Pankey Building Company, 8
GordonDunning, 207
Cindy Barganier of Cindy E. Barganier Interiors, LLC, back cover

To all those who brought this book to life—the incredibly talented art, writing, and photography team; the creative homeowners and brilliant designers who shared their inviting Southern spaces; and my Lord and Savior who has made all things beautiful—thank you. — K. WHALEY

*"A room should
start a conversation before
people actually start
exchanging words."*

— BARRY DIXON